10 Steps to Successfully Managing Recording Artists

D1566209

10 Steps to Successfully Managing Recording Artists

◆

A Guide to Effective Artist Management

Cappriccieo M. Scates, M.B.A.
(J.D. Candidate)

Foreword by
Nastacia "Nazz" Kendall
(DreamWorks Music Publishing)

iUniverse, Inc.
New York Lincoln Shanghai

10 Steps to Successfully Managing Recording Artists
A Guide to Effective Artist Management

All Rights Reserved © 2004 by Cappriccieo Montrell Scates

No part of this book may be reproduced or transmitted in any form or by any means, graphic, electronic, or mechanical, including photocopying, recording, taping, or by any information storage retrieval system, without the written permission of the publisher.

iUniverse, Inc.

For information address:
iUniverse, Inc.
2021 Pine Lake Road, Suite 100
Lincoln, NE 68512
www.iuniverse.com

International Standard Serial Number: 1551-8477

The information in this book represents the thoughts and opinions of the author. Therefore, they may not be applicable to all situations. As a result, the author and publisher indemnify themselves of any responsibilities for actions that may be taken by readers subsequent to the suggestions, ideas, statements, or thoughts offered in this book. Use caution before applying any of the information given, and always seek the advice of legal counsel.

ISBN: 0-595-32851-2

Printed in the United States of America

To Maya, Cappriccieo, Cappriccieo Jr., Moneticelle, Domonique, and Shalen

Helen Marie Lewis

In 1984, I received a typewriter from my grandmother for my 15th birthday. Truthfully, I was very disappointed and I couldn't figure out why she would buy me a typewriter. She had been telling me for months how much I was going to love my birthday present. Quite frankly, once I got it, I hated it and wanted to cry. For the most part, it took me about ten years from the day I got it to realize its true meaning and value.

Unfortunately, she died in 1995, and I never got the opportunity to say, "Momma I understand what you meant by giving me a typewriter and I am so grateful for your infinite wisdom and guidance." I Love You…

Anthony B. Spriggs

I'll never be able to truly thank you. It took a man and an angel from Heaven to do what you did for my son. RIP

***This book is also dedicated to all of those who came before me and broke apart the walls of adversity in order to make it possible for me, and others to pursue our dreams. It is a blessing to have the opportunities that we have today. Although, we still have a long way to go on many levels, we owe you an enormous amount of gratitude for your valuable and noteworthy efforts.

Contents

"If you think education is expensive, you should try ignorance."

"You have to know when to hold 'em and when to fold 'em."

"Plan your work and work your plan."

"There is no such thing as reality, there is only perception."

"The power of the tongue should never be taken lightly."

"Be prepared to get back less than you put out."

"Passion is no substitute for commitment."

"Drawing this line may require a needlepoint."

"Learn the importance of the After Action Review (AAR)."

Foreword

It was about March of 1999 in Hampton, Virginia and I was tending to my routine waitress tasks at Applebee's, when one of my co-workers rushed into the kitchen to inform me that there were two customers looking for female artists to be in their five girls R&B group who would later be known as *De5ire* (Desire). Me, being as unenthusiastic as I could be because of the phrase "girls group", which translated to me as "problems", agreed to go out and sing for them just out of amusement. You see back then it always seemed as if everyone in Virginia had "something" going on, but who other than Teddy Riley, Missy Elliot and Timberland really had it going on at the time?

Later, right before I graduated from high school with honors, an advanced studies diploma, and no true "*desire*" to pursue college, the local production team I came to know as Melodic Noiz Productions contacted me again and insisted that I come by their studio and tryout for their girls group. This time they were going to come by my house and pick me up so that I could not give them any excuse as to why I could not come, because they had been waiting for my arrival for three months since the time we initially met at Applebee's. I laughed, finally gave in, auditioned, and a new chapter of my life was being written right before my eyes entitled "Fate." I had no clue what God was planning for me, and especially what He had in store for my future the day after I was introduced to the group's manager, *Cappriccieo M. Scates.*

Here before me was a man with a vision of such optimism, intelligence and determination that I had never seen before. With my realistic perceptions on life and very little outlook on sacrificing for things not assured, I was so impressed and spellbound by Mr. Scates' radical nature. I often wondered how does he sleep at night? How could this man of five kids, a wife, dog, house, and three cars move on such impulse without apprehension? Never fearing the unknown, prepared for the outcome, and always willing to sacrifice the attention necessary to achieve and reach his true calling, which was undoubtedly artist management.

Needless to say, after a year of switching girls and finalizing the group, we received and signed a deal with Universal Records. Unfortunately, like the typical female group, we separated before the first vocal could be sung on our attempted single. Words were said, tears were shed, and everyone went their separate ways.

Cappriccieo encouraged me to keep exploring my options in the entertainment world by assisting me with appearances on (Soul Train, music videos, MTV dance shows, etc.), and I eventually found myself writing in Kay Gee's studio (Divine Mill/NJ; former member of Naughty by Nature). Throughout my journey in finding an alternative niche in the industry, I continued to confer with Cappriccieo in remembrance of how I always perceived him as more than just a gentleman "trying to keep the lights on," as I quote one of his many famous phrases. I witnessed his dedication, trustworthiness and agility. Witnessing his abilities made me realize that no one else could better represent me than he. So, we decided to officially form a manager/client relationship again.

Not only would this be one of the most important decisions of my new found career, but also the best decision of years to come, which would also incorporate managing me as an artist as he had done before. Though, we had gone through the trials and triumphs of De5ire, I knew he was more than capable of managing my career as a songwriter and in a short period of time proved this by securing a publishing deal with DreamWorks within a year.

Five years ago you could not have told me that I would have been a Billboard Award Winning Songwriter and that this man would be the one to send me on my way soaring to the top! A new interval would be created between the two of us and with our different aspects on faith in the "circus of life," we would soon have one of the best balancing acts of optimism and realism any artist and manager could ever imagine!

Throughout the years of knowing Cappriccieo, he has consistently proven himself as a credible manager and promoter in the music industry through his past accomplishments and present endeavors. Since the beginning stages of Precision Management in 1992, he has shown himself to be dedicated and determined to succeed. As a result, I appointed him as Vice President of my company—Nazz-E-Aten Publishing/Songs of DreamWorks (BMI). In doing so, we have accomplished the #1 Hit Single, "Feels Good (Don't Worry 'Bout A Thing)" by Naughty By Nature featuring 3LW, worked with recording artists such as: Syleena Johnson, Nivea, Mario, JoJo, Frankee, Jhane, CoKo of SWV, and collaborated with some of the industry's hottest producers such as: Kay Gee, Vincent Herbert, Troy Taylor, Malik Pendelton, Yogi, Bink, Chris Henderson, Kwame, Dent, Saint Nick, Lil' Ronnie, Teddy Riley, The Platinum Brothers, Daron of (112), Tyrice Jones, Pic Conley, and many others. Believe it or not, in the midst of all of this he has also managed to fit in law school and represent a production team known as the *Trend~Settas* who have covers on Syleena

Johnson, Nivea, Mario, Urban Mystic, Queen Latifah, The Beauty Shop Soundtrack, and The Cookout Soundtrack.

Clearly, Cappriccieo's combination of accomplishments, history, street-knowledge, and a Masters in Business Management, has proven his place in the music industry. His forever enduring spirit, passion for music, education, professionalism and dedication to the business and his clients helps create the reflection of the man he is and will become in building his legacy for his family that, in the end, no token or words of gratitude could ever amount to. He is a triumphant manager, husband, father, son, grandson, brother, uncle, nephew, friend of mine and child of God with the sword of valor, the eye of reliance and The Book of Wisdom to help shield, conquer and win victory over all and any obstacles that come his way. I am a proud living example of his strong will to survive in such an unforgiving industry and have taken on some of his tactics along the way. Not only is it apparent that God has shinned down on his very existence in this world and career choice, but his grandmother is forever smiling down on him as well, and would be very proud to have witnessed all of his success and blessings to come. It has been a pleasure and true honor working with Cappriccieo, and I'd advise anyone who picks up this book to read these 10 steps at his or her own discretion, apply them, and may God be with you on your journey into the world of artist management!

Nastacia "Nazz" Kendall
Nazz-E-Aten Publishing/Songs of DreamWorks (BMI)

Preface

Recent changes in the music industry have revolutionized the way we must approach artist management. This is a very different and unique time from years past. As managers, we must make it a point to explore various options and outlets for doing business. We have to learn to effectively manage every aspect of our clients' careers. If you are currently managing artists or contemplating management, you must give a great deal of thought and consideration to your responsibilities as a manager. Using a logical approach to artist management may be the face card, but being prepared and direct is a trump.

Many managers attempt to manage on impulse and assumptions. This can create an environment that is detrimental in nature. Managing artists without being able to clearly assess and objectively evaluate your plans and abilities is seemingly inconceivable. However, I have witnessed managers attempting to do so during my entire career. The manager/client relationship is an agreement or promise on your part to effectively advise and counsel your clients. It is a bond, charging you to perform those duties to the best of your abilities. As a result of my observations, I was inspired to write this book with hopes that I can assist my fellow colleagues by providing them with 10 simple, but effective steps to successfully representing their clients. I am also hopeful that this book will serve as a guide and point of reference for artists and industry professionals looking to assess or evaluate the characteristics of a competent manager or management firm.

Overall, I sincerely hope that this book serves to channel you to heights beyond your imagination. Whether you desire to become more successful at artist management, are trying to enhance your current approach, or have just started managing, this book may help you to design or review your tactics. First-rate and accomplished management is central to the careers of artists. Good solid management tactics for maintaining and sustaining your clients' careers will be essential. Moreover, good management—or the lack thereof—may often prove to be crucial. In fact, I closed two major deals during the time that I was writing this book by applying the very exact principles enclosed.

Management may always be a point for review and may involve a specifically defined level of extreme, high accountability. You should always welcome the challenges that management may bring, and always be prepared to put forth a maximum effort. Your success may be forthcoming. I beckon you to move forward with zeal and resolve during your quest on the road of artist management; it awaits you.

Cappriccieo M. Scates, M.B.A. (J.D. Candidate)
Author

Acknowledgments

There have been so many people that have contributed to my success over the years that I am a bit reluctant to make specific acknowledgments in fear that I may leave a name or two out, which is not consistent with my heart. So, if I miss a name or two, or don't say as much as you think I should about "**YOU**" please don't hold it against me.

First and foremost, I'd like to thank God for continually helping me to reach new depths and for never letting me down. My mom always told me that You would never close a door without opening a window first. Thanks for making me skinny enough to fit through those windows (TYJ).

Maya, thanks for being you and for being one hell of a woman. You are evidence that I am in God's Favor and have helped me to prove to everyone that, "I know a star when I see one."

To my children CP, Pig, Nay Nay, Domonique, and Shalen, it is through you that I live forever. Thanks for always letting me know that I am loved and deserve to be called Dad.

Mom, thanks for your undying love and commitment. You've told me since a small child that I could write and I should take it seriously. Well, I finally listened!

Shermarrcco, I was once told that you only get three good women in your life. You pushed me over the limit a long time ago!

Dad, I waited so long to find you, and I am glad to have the opportunity that we have to move forward. I hope I turned out to be a son that you are truly proud of.

To my newly found sisters, I fell in love with you instantly!

My grandfather James, uncles, aunts, nephews, cousins, nieces, in-laws, and friends, without you I am nothing. Honestly, the words thank you will never be enough for what each of you have meant to me. So, please accept those two words with the understanding that they come from the bottom of my heart and know that you have each provided me with the platform to develop and grow. For that, I will forever be grateful!

Nazz, thanks for being apart of the vision and for helping to validate my management skills. I know you want all the bases covered so, here is your S for the

Serious times, your P for the growing Pains, the E for Every moment during the journey, don't forget your C for Comfort, the I for Intangible, your A for Abundance, and an L for Longevity. You have been a true Godsend, and very S-P-E-C-I-A-L during my journey. Thank You, Thank You, Thank You, for so many things. Please know that I appreciate everything that you have done…Keep doing what you do. You are truly, "THAT GIRL!"

Joe'i, thanks for always appreciating me, and for showing your respect and gratitude for my abilities.

Trend~Settas, thanks for keeping me on my toes, you guys have always kept me preparing for the next question.

Pic Conley, Nat Martin, and Bobby Duckett, thanks for being my industry mentors and shining examples of true professionalism.

Vincent McFarlane, you were there as my partner from the very beginning. Although we don't speak as much anymore, I haven't forgotten your valued friendship.

Darius Brooks, thanks for the many lessons in God. Each time I am around you I pay close attention to your every word because you speak the truth according to the Word.

Anthony G. Davis (the G is for_____) thanks for looking out and congrats on your accomplishments. I look up to you!

Thanks, Darryl Lindsey you gave me my first (paid) start in the business of artist marketing and promotions from back in the Atlantic days. So, it's all your fault!

Thanks for helping me to keep the lights on—Kevin Black (you are the best to ever do this!), Dick Scott (thanks for sharing your insight with me), Troy Marshall, Garnet Reid, Steve Stein, Scott Johnson, Sam Crespo, Chris Atlas, Jamal Elledge (we'll figure out something) Russ Regan, Jason Windborne, Chris Swartz, Kevin Glickman, Joe "The Butcher" Nicolo, Rose Mann, Jeff Wells, Mustafaa Shabazz, Malik Levy (thanks for teaching me that I was in the game When I didn't realize it) Cool Dre, Tyrone Clerk, Phil Thornton, Everett "Jam" Benton, Nadir Smith, Tye Dash, Reg Reg (keep cutting those checks), Teddy Riley, Big Paul & Brian Simpson/Blueprint, Big Shorty, Laudelyn Donehower, Bryan Leech, Greg Peck, Andy Anderson, Leotis Clyburn, Clive Davis (thanks for telling me to up my game), Barry Gordy, Al Bell, Lonnie Simmons, Surge Knight (man, you kept a lot of food on plenty of tables!), Jeff Thomas, Leesa Brunson, Susan Blond and staff, Luke, Dawn Capper, Theresa Rouge, Arthur Austin, Justin/Mark and the entire Spirit Music Group Family, John Gore, Debow, Kimmora Lee Simmons, Gordon "Apache" Collins (my true friend),

John Austin, Carlton, Screwface, Tony "Chubbz" Marcus, Troy Taylor (how's your pool and fence coming?), Slim Tim, Mi-L, Men of Our Time, KP, Strong, Naughty By Nature, Bink, Guy, JoJo, Vincent Herbert, Frankee, All-Star Gordon, D2 Management, Platinum Brothers, A.D. Washington, Avery Lewis, Fat Tommy, Montrell Million (thanks for keeping me inspired), Tammy Tisdale, David Broom, Kay Gee & Dee Dee/Divine Mill, Sean Williams, Ty (my street team dog), Maurice Edison (you held Richmond down for me), Mickey Benzo, Michael Selverne (I wanna be just like you when I grow up), David Gold, my friends at BMI, my friends at ASCAP, Kimberly Archie and my friends at AFTRA, all my friends at radio and retail that I worked with over the years, all my club DJ's and club owners, my mix-tape cats, and my video folks. You have all been extremely important to my career.

I'd also like to thank all of the artists and industry professionals that I've had the opportunity to work with throughout my career. Having the opportunity to work with so many talented and creative people has been a blessing, and I am a true fan and admirer of each of you. There is nothing like being in the same company of those whom you admire.

I'd like to thank my college professors and fellow classmates for a wonderful and very valuable exchange of insight and knowledge. MBA 420 you are each, "representative samples" of greatness! Thanks, LA, Randall, J.D., and Al our connection is forever!

Finally, I'd like to salute all of my friends that I served with while in the U.S. Army and the U.S. Army National Guard. It was a great place to start!

P.S.

If you have ever known me as, or referred to me as Don, you are truly one of my favorite persons in this whole world, and I LOVE YOU DEARLY!

Shawn, I know you went through the fire many times. I hope you eventually find a nice cool lake with unrestricted swimming.

Thanks Angel Potter, John Kellogg, and Felisha Booker for inspiring me to write this…

Introduction

Whenever people ask, "What do managers do?" I'm tempted to answer, "What *don't* they do?" By definition, management involves the process of treating with care, exercising executive, administrative, and supervisory direction, and succeeding in accomplishing a task while supervising something (as a business). Overall, a manager's job entails key responsibilities that are closely related to planning, organizing, directing, guiding, and controlling the careers of artists. Managers can advise their clients on almost any subject—from musical projects, to personal relationships, to buying a car. Artist managers play a crucial role in building the careers of artists, and this book will outline what I consider to be the 10 most important steps involved with managing an artist's career. During my 15 years as an artist manager in the music industry, I have developed this 10-step process, which you can use to establish or enhance your artist management business. Overall, they can be used as footstools towards your own personal and professional destiny. As you read through each chapter, you will gain a new or better understanding of what successful artist management is all about, and you'll also learn the importance of putting these steps into operation. Knowing how to organize and administrate an artist's career to its full potential is of utmost importance to your overall success as a manager.

A good manager can assist an artist to phenomenal heights, just as a bad one can send an artist's career into nonexistence. Managers come from various backgrounds and serve as liaisons for their clients. They provide a number of functions that are essential to the careers of artists. These functions include—but are not limited to—negotiating deals, assisting with tour/show coordination, selecting attorneys and other team members, supervising the day-to-day operational requirements, and selecting material such as songs, photos, styles, and outlines/plans. Artists employ managers to advise and counsel them and to insure that their careers and interests are being properly managed. As a result, it's important that the manager be skilled and knowledgeable in areas specific to the needs of the artist and his or her career. In many instances, management can be likened to the responsibilities of parenting, and is therefore an extremely delicate and vital perspective of an artist's career. Artist management is very personal in nature and requires that you be committed to providing aggressive and cutting edge services while maintaining the integrity and ultimate survival and success of your clients.

Managers need to provide their clients with structure, direction, and insight, while progressively advancing the market value of their clients' careers. Managers will also need to be committed to assuring a high quality, goal-oriented, and personalized system where their clients can thrive and excel through the manager's knowledge, experience, and ability to apply the 10 steps outlined in this book. Overall, it is the manager's job to meet and exceed industry standards by propelling their clients to the forefront of today's marketplace. Every artist or talent in the industry is in need of effective and competent management. This book is about the steps needed to be effective as a manager as a result of providing the management services required to get the job done.

Objectivity and Subjectivity

"If you think education is expensive, you should try ignorance."

Often, artists are not as savvy when it comes to selecting their managers and representatives as managers need to be when making choices and key decisions relating to their careers. That's why it is very important for managers to be aware of key areas in which they will need to be familiar in order to reach their desired goals. Education has always been the key to success. In fact, you can never know too much about your profession of choice. The more you know about it, the better off you are. Education breeds objectivity by providing you with insight and diversity and helps you make informed decisions. It also helps to provide you with various opportunities and options that may otherwise be closed as a result of your lack of knowledge. Typically, the less you know the more you have to rely on the knowledge of others, which makes you subject to what you are being told—right or wrong. Taking the time to educate yourself assures that you will be better prepared to represent and effectively manage your clients. Education is a continual process and you will never stop learning new and more effective ways to conduct business.

You should study and learn as much as you can about the inner workings of record companies, production companies, publishing companies, performing rights organizations, and various other companies, as they will relate to your client's career. A large amount of your education can be gained through networking with various other managers and industry professionals. Networking can be central to learning and educating yourself as it relates to artist management. It is a good practice to interact with other managers as a source for information and knowledge. Depending on your specific situation, it may also be a good idea to form partnerships with other management firms in order to utilize the experience, education, and resources of those firms.

Overall, read, research, and learn as much as you can about the music industry and the profession of artist management. Don't be afraid to ask questions or admit you are not familiar with a particular area. Never fully subject yourself to the thoughts and ideas of others without arming yourself with the ability to challenge or object, based on your own knowledge and insight. This will be gained over time, with experience, and through education. As with most things, practice makes perfect. However, attempting to manage someone without at least educating yourself in as many areas as possible may prove to be disastrous. Quite frankly, managing someone's career and livelihood is no place for lackadaisical on-the-job training.

You should be willing to compromise with other team members. Don't become one-dimensional as a result of your education. There is always more than one way of doing things. Specifically, utilize your education and knowledge to enhance your overall ability to get the job done, and not as a hindrance to your clients or other members of your team because of your inability or unwillingness to accept other points of view. Your ability to function as a goal-oriented team player will prove to be important to your client's success and growth.

In addition, always welcome the assistance of others and take the time to learn from each and every situation, whether it's good, bad, or indifferent. The world of artist management will provide you with numerous amounts of hands-on knowledge and education. Coupled with your readings and research, you can ultimately develop a management style and consistency that may be revered by your clients, peers, and various members of the entertainment community. Your education and objectivity will assist you with the overall process of management and provide you with the insight necessary to properly manage, select, develop, and cultivate talent.

Selection and Rejection

"You have to know when to hold 'em and when to fold 'em."

Your job will require far more than just riding on tour buses and having fun. Therefore, there are a number of things that you should consider when determining whether or not to take on a particular client. Choosing which clients not to work with is equally as important as choosing the ones that you decide to work with. Knowing the types of artists that are suitable for your style of management is very important. Just because someone is talented doesn't mean that he or she is manageable or fits your particular vision and style of management. It is important that you select artists that you totally believe in, because the artists you select are extensions of you and should be reflective of your reputation and abilities. Most importantly, you should be honest with yourself during the selection process by knowing your own capabilities as they relate to being able to facilitate a particular artist specifically.

Obviously, you will need to assess the talents of your potential clients. Selecting the right clients is somewhat of a gamble. However, during your management career you will eventually hone your skills to a point where you will be able to access a potential client's current or future market value within the first 5-10 minutes of meeting him or her with a considerable degree of certainty. Having the ability to correctly access talent can be key to sustaining your management career. You should never settle for mediocrity over substance. Nevertheless, you may note that the industry has evolved into a business where marketing over substance is customary. Yet I must caution, even the best marketing in the world won't stimulate a consumer to purchase a poor product more than once. For that reason, your chances of being successful are far greater if you manage and market quality artists and projects.

Determining a potential client's marketability will be a decision based on your impression of them and your understanding of the current or projected market trends. Though it is more the exception than the norm, it is not unusual for managers to be ahead of trends and select artists whom they feel will be in demand during a future time period. In general, managers select clients based on current trends and their beliefs in their own abilities to effectively represent the interests of that particular client. Each artist may be unique and require his or her own specialized system. Moreover, most artists require a great deal of attention and time devoted to their specific needs. Keep in mind that management is personal in nature, and therefore, you will want to consider those artists who appear manageable and akin to the types of clients that you desire to represent. Originality, credits, dedication, self-confidence, and professionalism will all be the types of things that dictate and determine your decisions regarding client representation.

Your search for talent will require that you make yourself available by identifying yourself as a manager and proclaiming your position as a seeker of talent. You will quickly discover that there are a large number of people that consider themselves artists or feel that they have the talent required to succeed in the music industry. Therefore, finding prospective clients won't be your main issue, but finding *good ones* will! In addition, you should list yourself and your company via outlets such as *The Songwriter's Market, The Recording Industry Source Book, The Hollywood Music Industry Directory*, and all available publications and interactive arenas that cater to established and aspiring artists. This will help expose you to talent from all over the world and provide you with an outlet for stabilizing or discovering talent.

You should also set and establish criteria for the types of clients that show interest in your services and for those you will be seeking as well. This will help you to quickly evaluate and eliminate those that are not consistent with your desired specifications. You should remain professional and courteous at all times while in the presence of talent you are reviewing. Good business ethics and principles will go a long way when you are establishing new contacts or attempting to sustain current and future relationships. The impressions you make will have long-lasting effects on your success and productivity. Keep in mind the music industry is a creative arena, filled with creative people. Therefore, your ability to demonstrate and articulate your respect and understanding of creativity is a must. The clients you select or reject will almost always be emotionally expressive, sensitive, original thinkers, positive, youthful, and nonconformists.

As a result, you will need to develop methods that will afford you the opportunity to provide constructive criticism to those whom you reject by encouraging them and providing them with suggestions that may improve their skills or material. In addition, there may be times when you are fond of a particular artist, but just don't feel that you can effectively represent their particular needs. In these cases, you may consider finding ways to direct them towards other contacts that may be able to service their particular needs. Usually, your input will be greatly appreciated and may help an aspiring artist to do well in the future; even if you ultimately decide not to represent him or her. Finding clients that are manageable and want to be managed by way of your direction is very important. In fact, it may be more important to find clients that possess the ability to learn and take direction than it is finding those with the most talent. On the other hand, if you find that you are interested in representing a particular talent, but do not feel that he or she is fully developed to industry standards; you should take the time to nurture and develop their skills. You should work to familiarize him or her with what is required to succeed in the music industry, and attempt to help him or her to achieve success by working together as a team.

There is no way to guarantee success as a manager, but setting standards and having sound administrative and decision-making skills during your selection process will definitely increase your chances of success. It is important to be as realistic and optimistic as possible during the selection process. However, never overlook the possibility of falling short of your desired outcome. Making the right choices and selections will be the benchmark of your management career. Your ability to adapt, generate, and regenerate your choices by way of planning for various possibilities can be beyond measure. Establishing and creating a system for effective selection and implementation of your plans is important. Subsequently, creating direct and indirect approaches during your stages of selection will prove to be helpful. Your need to plan as a manager is a natural precondition to establishing good plans and selecting the right clients. Planning is timeless and especially important to a good management and selection system.

Planning and Implementation

"Plan your work and work your plan."

Having the ability to multitask and properly plan could greatly impact your management career. Duties such as handling publicity, promotions, and finances, as well as managing your contacts and juggling various other aspects can be a direct indication of your ability to multitask and plan. Planning is about setting objectives and deciding how to reach those objectives. Therefore, planning should not only be about future decisions, but rather about how the decisions you make today will impact the future. Setting objectives through planning may provide you with markers to gauge your overall success and effectiveness. Your objectives should be clear, concise, and detailed to the point that you, your team, and your clients can identify them. They should also be written, relevant, measurable, prioritized, updated on a regular basis, and realistic. You should review, research, and exhaust all possibilities during the planning process.

Plans should always forecast activities and set outlines that will assist to build long and successful careers for your clients. In order to succeed in management, you will need to have a systematic approach and plan, which may help to eliminate the guesswork. When establishing your plans, you should consider the who's, what's, where's, when's, and how's. Establishing who, what, where, when, and how may help you create a system that will outline each stage of your plan. You should consider things such as: who should do what as it relates to the plan, what exactly needs to be done, and what actions need to be taken to get it done? Also consider, where will you find the resources to accomplish your plan and what methods or procedures will you use? In addition, consider when it should be done and what your timeframe is. Then finally, ask, how will you approach accomplishing your plan and how will you effectively accomplish your objective?

Keep in mind that each situation and client will be different, and thus may require a varied or specialized approach. You will need to develop a system and points of reference that will establish your general rules, polices, and procedures as they relate to planning. It is imperative that you learn not to pursue objectives that become obscured and obsolete. A large portion of planning has to do with your ability to assess and establish the correct and least resistant routes for reaching your preferred objectives. Always keep your plans open for review and analysis. Your plans should be definitive and specific, with no general interpretations. A defined plan is essential to all functions of business. Most importantly, you should also have backup and contingency plans in place, regardless of how thorough your initial plans are. During your planning stages, you will note that there may be occasions when you may need to reconstruct your plans due to unforeseen or unpredictable occurrences. A sudden mandatory meeting, downtime, or a dry spell could arise that may result in your need to create an alternate plan to assist you with reaching your goals and objectives.

At any rate, always be prepared to deal with the potential for these types of occurrences, and keep your clients updated as often as possible regarding any shifts or changes to your plans that may be required. Your ability to plan for various situations will also reflect your ability to handle the day-to-day operations of your client's careers. In addition, you should also factor in the need to plan for assisting your clients with the possibility of avoiding outside influences that may possibly divert his or her focus. More than likely, there will always be someone external to your firm, attempting to advise your clients contrary to the plans and guidelines that you and your team may establish. Be prepared to answer or reject their challenges. Keep an eye out for potentially detrimental plan intervention as a result of your client's family members, friends, associates, or loved ones. In most instances, your contractual agreement with your clients will make provisions to protect you against potential backlashes as a result of your client's concentration towards negative influences. For the most part, you may find this issue to be constant, and often adverse to your plans. You should always advise your clients against adhering to negative influences that may affect your plans, such as drugs, excessive alcohol, and various behavioral or mind altering addictions.

On a more personal note, another part of your plan should factor the need to attempt to keep your clients healthy by monitoring and recommending proper diets, exercise, and regular doctor visits. You should also ask your clients frequently about their health and mental status. This may help to keep your clients physically and mentally fit, which will be important to your overall plans and objectives for them. Furthermore, you should always attempt to assist your clients with planning for and maintaining the five necessities in life, which are food, clothing, shelter, transportation, and communication. These will be key areas specifically related to your client's physical, emotional, and mental attributes, and will factor in greatly to the success of your overall plans.

Though attempting to keep your personal interests separate from those of your clients will be difficult while planning, your objective should be to satisfy the interests of your clients, and not your own. However, a good plan will often satisfy your interests as well. Not all of your clients will grow at the same pace or be on the same levels. As your relationships develop, being able to manage and maintain your clients' careers will be your ultimate responsibility. Whether your client is a new artist, or one who is established with a long and successful career, your job will be to maintain and keep him or her stable throughout. Again, the way you plan and prepare for this task is critical. It is often far more difficult to maintain something than it is to obtain it. However, artist management should seem as simple as possible from the artist's standpoint so they can stay focused and at ease. Consequently, they may not need to know, or even be interested in every intricate detail of your plan. As a result, you may consider making him or her aware of their specific duties and responsibilities only.

The importance of planning and executing your plans thereafter can factor into every decision that you make for your client's career. This is a key area of responsibility and shouldn't ever be delegated. A good and well thought out plan can serve as a millstone to the success of your client's careers. The way you plan and establish your plans will be particularly important to your success and professional reputation. In fact, you can never be too prepared or spend too much time developing a plan. Your reputation and survival will be determined by perception and how well you appear to have things set and planned in the proper perspective. Once you have established your reputation, it will follow you throughout your career. This fact should be key to your outlook and help to emphasize the importance of planning. It should also help illustrate to you how your ability to plan will affect your career and reputation as a whole. Use your ability to plan to set the tone for your reputation. It is a skill that will define your reputation and how you are perceived throughout your career.

Reputation and Misconception

"There is no such thing as reality, there is only perception."

A major part of professional business involves goodwill and the way others perceive you as a result of how you treat them. In fact, your reputation is often based on perception only. It is safe to say that managers who spend time studying and seriously thinking about their overall professional perception have a more useful basis for making decisions regarding their appearance and reputation than those who have not. Your reputation and personal integrity are sensitive subjects and should be handled with extreme care and attention. In addition, professional etiquette and ethics should always be held in the highest esteem as they relate to your reputation. Generally, practicing good etiquette and ethics will be consistent with profitability and your reputation. However, doing what you believe is right and ethical may not always satisfy your own personal interests. As you grow in your career, you will be able to reflect on and understand ethical lessons you may be taught that may help your ability to refine and modify your principles and practices along the way.

Your ability to keep your reputation in tact will be a superb challenge, but it can be successfully obtained. Subsequently, the nature of the music industry may serve to challenge and attempt to sway your principle guidelines. In particular, be as honest and forthright as possible. Never attempt to manipulate or mislead your clients. It is not consistent with good business practices and ethics, and it may have a lasting negative affect on your reputation. Being approachable and respectable to others can also serve to enhance your reputation and the way others perceive you. Throughout you career, you may be faced with all sorts of challenges related to artist management. A good reputation can help to minimize the difficulties of those challenges. Therefore, it is important that you never compromise your reputation as a result of doing something unethical and against the principles you establish for yourself, your company, and your clients.

When an artist engages a manager, it is usually done on an exclusive basis, thus the artist is exclusive to the manager. However, the manager is almost never exclusive to the artist, and thus is free to manage and represent other clients.

Consequently, managers can fall short of their responsibilities as a result of taking on more clients than they can effectively represent, which may damage their overall reputation as a result. Your clients should remain your primary focus throughout the term of each agreement. Your chances of success may be infinitesimal, and a lack of focus will almost always impede your chances of success. By and large, the more focused you are on your clients, the harder you will work at reaching your management goals, and thereby improve your status and reputation amongst your clients and associates.

In general, over the course of your career there may be misunderstandings or misinterpretations that can often reflect your clients' understandings of what your duties consist of. Often, this may affect their perception and your reputation as a whole. It will be your job to correctly express and outline your responsibilities so your clients are fully informed and don't get a skewed view of what your duties are. For example, one of the biggest misconceptions that artists have regarding managers is they often believe that managers should function as banks by bankrolling their careers. Although, managers often make financial investments and contributions, it is normally not their responsibility to financially facilitate the careers of their clients. Overall, the manager's ultimate job is to advise and counsel, and not to be a financial partner. However, you may find yourself carrying out and performing many duties that are not consistent with your job title.

In fact, you may find yourself taking on many of your clients' personal burdens as a result of your focus and drive to see your clients succeed.

From time to time you may even notice your clients shifting the weight of their individual responsibilities to you. Although, you should make it a point to acknowledge and express your interests in your clients continued survival, you may need to steer him or her in a direction away from filling your job with issues that may otherwise divert your focus and cause you to be less effective. The job of management will require a team effort from your clients as well. It should not be one directional. Therefore, try not to get caught in the misconception and misinterpretation of what your function as a manager specifically calls for.

Your overall character and management customs will define how your clients and other industry professionals view you. Having a solid ethical base to start with can rapidly increase your growth and reflect well on your overall reputation. It will be important that you find ways to separate your clients' personal and professional needs and define your position so that your clients don't develop misconceptions of what is to be expected. Overall, you may find this point helpful with gaining the status and respect that you may desire from your clients. Furthermore, your overall reputation and the way you are perceived will also have to do with your ability to utilize the proper discretion. Knowing what to say, when to say it, and how to correct something you or your client may have said is fundamental. The power of words and word selection will be essential to your ability to negotiate on behalf of your clients. It is important that you get to know each person that you will be dealing with in order to solidify your reputation and aid with your discretionary approach.

Discretion and Regression

"The power of the tongue should never be taken lightly."

The ability to use discretion when dealing with various people may be the most important and underrated step of all listed. This is a skill that will permeate throughout your entire management career. Relying on impulse and instinct will generally lead to hasty decisions that may often prompt indiscretion. Therefore, acting impulsively without calculation can lead to some of the biggest mistakes when making decisions regarding your clients. Before embarking on any situation, take the time to gather your thoughts and prepare the words necessary to reach your desired outcome. You will quickly realize that there is no substitute for being prepared and armed with considerable knowledge once you have formed your own patterns for discretionary communication.

Taken as a whole, discretion should be factored into your management system to a point where you can move about using a large degree of prudence so effortlessly that it becomes second nature to you. Discretion is closely related to timing, and is therefore greatly affected by order and structure. The more in order and structured your operation, the better the chances that you will be able to appropriately employ discretion. The difference between success and failure in the entertainment industry can hinge on your ability to account for timing and discretion.

The success of your career may largely be based on your network, the relationships you form, and your ability to cultivate them throughout the years. Since there are so many different people and personalities in this world, you can never think that everyone is the same or will react in the same manner. Being prepared and knowing how to decipher the personalities of people by way of discretion is of the essence. When corresponding with your acquaintances, you should attempt to learn when to remain discreet and how to stay humble. This ability can also be central to enhancing your career. You should always attempt to be as discreet as possible with those external to your firm regarding your plans or what you are working towards. It may not be necessary to make everyone aware of everything that's happening. This may be important for a number of reasons.

Specifically, you may never know who is or is not supportive of your plans and objectives. Not using the proper discretion and exposing specific information to the wrong sources may prove to be damaging. In addition, keep in mind that things do not always turn out as planned. As a result, being discreet may also help you to remain humble and at the same time protect your client's career, which will also reflect your own. Using discretion and withholding information about your firm's activities and those of your clients can also help sustain a good reputation. In essence, it is significant that you be particular with what information you decide to share, and with whom.

You should be cognizant of the fact that just about everyone you encounter along the way can prove to have some value in the long run. Therefore, never burn a bridge if you can help it. However, should this situation occur, you should also know how to humble yourself in attempts to mend a burned bridge. Recognizing key people or the importance of a particular outing for your clients is imperative. There is nothing wrong with asking someone to excuse an action that you may have taken inappropriately. In fact, your ability to do so can be a plus towards your reputation and can ultimately have a positive effect for your clients and their careers. At times, artist management may be a thankless job whereby you have to be prepared to bear the brunt of every good or bad decision alike. Keep in mind, a good contingency plan can prove to be useful for a situation requiring regression and recovery.

Overall, your capability to handle each situation discreetly may be the personification of your expertise and experience throughout the entire music industry. Your ability to be discreet and utilize regression may also serve as a barometer for your level of integrity and professionalism. You should never underestimate the power or necessity of discretion. Be prepared to make use of it at all times when attempting to preserve or gain business relationships. Your usage and understanding of discretion can help secure and solidify your position within the industry as a whole. It can also assist you with securing and procuring talent. Accordingly, the more you invest in your ability to use discretion, the more it may help to facilitate you with securing your management career.

Deposit and Security

"Be prepared to get back less than you put out."

Artist management can be a lifetime commitment. There may be no real security in a business that is unusually risky by nature. Consequently, be geared up and prepared for the long haul of the many ups and downs you may encounter along the way. You are almost certain to earn much less monetarily than you actually put into the business. This fact may quickly become apparent, especially during the early stages of your management career. In most instances, you may never get what you deserve; only what you are able to negotiate.

Generally, managers receive a commission of 15%-25% of their clients' gross earnings, plus reimbursement for travel and out-of-pocket expenses. However, this may vary as a result of a number of factors. Try not to be too trivial over money, but know how and when you are to be paid. You should attempt to insure that you are paid at the time your clients are paid, and from their gross earnings, not their net. Your clients' earnings may fluctuate from time to time, and as a courtesy you may find it appropriate to altar your commissioning cycle or fees to assist with his or her ability to maintain. This should be strictly done at your discretion and approved by each particular client. Should it become necessary to alter your commissioning cycle, you should consider alternative methods of compensation such as clauses that may give you an option to be paid as a member of the act, or by formulating other agreements or partnerships with those clients. Obviously, this may increase your responsibilities, but it may also provide you with more stake and interest in future success, which may help to account for your need to adjust your commissioning cycle.

You should pay very close attention to protecting the interests of your clients. In essence, when your clients' interests are protected, yours should be as well. Be mindful of the fact that it is your ultimate responsibility to oversee the well-being of your clients. As a result, your clients may place high regard and confidence in your capabilities. The slightest dereliction of duties on your part may be harmful to your clients' livelihood, which in turn may affect your overall disposition.

Making firm commitments to your clients' survival and appropriate decisions in the process could be the best deposit you ever make towards your own career.

You should make it a point to protect your company's interests by way of a legally documented management agreement with your clients. Be sure to follow those duties specified within the agreement to the letter, and always be attentive to the guidelines within. Hopefully, you won't find yourself involved in any legal disputes with your clients. However, your efforts to maintain the veracity of your contracts may fair well if you do. Your company's tax and corporate structure will be an important aspect to your overall success and security as well. Be sure to structure your company in such a manner that it will be beneficial to you in both the short and long run. In addition, you should learn as much as you can about investing. Certificates of deposits, mutual funds, real estate, stocks, bonds, and other business ventures may all be key to your security and ability to effectively represent your clients. Having good credit and a solid foundation can also help reduce some of the outside forces relating to capital that may affect your security and your ability to get the job done.

Your ability to work hard and deposit unequivocal determination and dedication may be the best security of success you will ever have. In fact, it will serve as your deposit towards your career. You may often be required to display an undying commitment through your dedication to the success of your clients and your determination to see their careers thrive. This may require you to be exceedingly motivated and virtually unstoppable in your quest to effectively manage and represent your clients. Your capacity to get motivated and stay motivated may be immeasurable.

Motivation and Dedication

"Passion is no substitute for commitment."

Management will require a great deal of motivation, determination, and dedication on your part. You may find yourself facing several difficult and challenging tasks. As a result, it will be imperative for you to remain steadfast and unaffected by the many adversities you may face. Though at times your goals may seem unobtainable, your motivation and commitment to reaching your goals will help you fair well in a difficult climate. Despite the fact that being motivated is important, it will not supercede the discipline necessary to remain dedicated and committed to your overall objectives. Again, by and large your plan should dictate and outline those specific requirements related to the time that should be dedicated to a particular objective. Your ability to remain dedicated and disciplined with regards to reaching your goals will be vital.

Taken as a whole, you may want to view motivation and dedication as one in the same. They will both be equally important to reaching your goals and objectives. Accordingly, you may spend an abundant amount of time applying your efforts equally towards both. Generally, as your career develops you may seek various avenues to stimulate you in each area. This fact will be consistent with your growth, accomplishments, and insight as they relate to your desire to reach and set different goals and objectives. Keeping a good positive and optimistic outlook will also be helpful regarding your ability to remain motivated and dedicated. Be mindful that your clients may often look to you as a source for motivation and dedication for their own confidence as well. Most often, they will expect you to keep a positive viewpoint and cheer them on along the way. Your strength, wisdom, and fortitude in the areas of motivation and dedication will be of extreme importance to your ability to nurture and sustain your client relations. Hence, you need to remain as motivated and dedicated as possible.

In order to continue being motivated and dedicated, it may require you to take a very humble approach to managing your clients. In fact, you may need to be content with allowing them to receive all the praises and acclaim, even when you do most of the work in the process. In fact, you may consider this approach similar to your lying over a puddle of water so that your clients can walk on your back without getting their feet wet, and not even getting a towel to dry yourself afterwards. Don't let these situations offend you. Keep in mind that status is often the enemy of success. You will need to be able to see your success through your clients' accomplishments unselfishly. Overall, you should try to keep their interests above your own as much as possible. This will be an important aspect regarding your ability to remain motivated and dedicated towards reaching your goals and objectives. Being able to see your clients' accomplishments as your own may be a required skill.

In general, there may be several times when you are required to utilize this skill. Your ability to do so may be an ultimate testament to your motivation, determination, and loyalty towards your clients as a whole. Furthermore, it will be important for you to establish a loyalty base between you and your clients. Your loyalty will weigh heavily on your ability to remain motivated and dedicated to your clients' well-being. Again, in general, if your clients are secure, so are you. Thus the more motivated and dedicated you are regarding your clients' careers, the more it will reflect positively on your own interests. You should always remain as committed to your clients as possible, and never allow your loyalty and dedication to be questioned.

Loyalty and Ambition

"Drawing this line may require a needlepoint."

Imagine yourself waiting at a bus stop for a bus. In particular, you have been waiting for this bus for about 3 hours. As a result, you are over an hour and a half late for your destination, and to top it off, it has just started raining. Of course you are not prepared for the rain because you didn't pay any attention to the forecast. Therefore, needless to say, you are even more anxious now for your bus to arrive than you were 2 minutes ago. Finally, you step into the street again, attempting to look down the road to see your bus as you have been doing for the past 3 hours. Fortunately, this time you can see the bus headlights about 4 blocks away. Instantly, you began to get even more restless and filled with ambitious thoughts about what you are going to do once your bus finally arrives to pick you up. The closer this bus gets, the more ambitious you get.

At last, the bus you have been waiting on for over 3 hours finally arrives, and just as you are about to set foot on that bus someone grabs your arm and says "Don't get on that bus; it's not the right one." The truth is, it is in fact a bus headed in a direction appearing to be going your way, but someone is telling you that it is the wrong bus. The bus driver is saying "Come on, let's go," and your first thought is motivated through your ambition, which tells you to get on the bus. However, someone is telling you not to get on the bus and that you need to trust their instincts. This person wants you to be loyal to them and to respect their point of view because they feel they are telling you what's in your best interest. Unfortunately, you are plagued with the fact that you have been waiting for so long for this moment, it's difficult for you to see this person's point of view. For the most part, all you see is the bus driver and your opportunity to finally get on the bus. The question is, do you get on the bus and follow your ambition, or do you decide to be loyal and take that person's advice and wait for the next bus?

Typically, there is a fine line between loyalty and ambition, thus it's hard for most people to remain loyal when they are ambitious. Generally, there isn't any harm or ill intent on the behalf of the person that decides to choose ambition over loyalty. However, he or she is usually driven to a point that affects their ability to rationalize things in such a manner that would otherwise cause them to be more considerate of others. You should be prepared for clients that will have difficulties choosing loyalty over ambition as it may relate to them having to make a specific decision, requiring them to be more loyal than their own ambitions and desires allot for.

Be that as it may, you should always attempt to keep your clients cognizant of the fact that you are aware of their ambitions by continually showing your loyalty and commitment to satisfying their specific goals. Although there is no way to specifically account for loyalty verses ambition, the more involved you are with your clients' goals and aspirations, the more trust and loyalty may be established. Keeping your clients loyal and responsive to the overall plan and objective will have a tremendous impact on your success as a manager. Overall, your clients' ambition may serve to keep you focused and attentive to their specific needs. It may also help to identify those areas of your clients' careers that they are most concerned with. Their ambition should be reviewed and discussed as a part of your overall plan. It should also be greatly considered during the feedback and follow-up process.

More than likely, your attentiveness to your clients' ambitions and desires will prove to be the crux of your relationship. You should attempt to utilize this fact to your advantage by always being mindful of the dilemma artists often find themselves in when it comes to loyalty and ambition, and the choices within. Utilize feedback to assess your clients' ambitions, and always attempt to show your concerns for their well-being.

Feedback and Follow-up

"Learn the importance of the After Action Review (AAR)."

A large portion of communication involves feedback and your ability to exchange ideas and information. It also requires you to be an effective listener with a keen sense and openness for various points of view. You should know how to take the time to listen, and always keep information as accurate as possible. To be effective, feedback must flow as an exchange of information and ideas between you and your clients. Your clients may have a number of questions, so be prepared to field their concerns. You should establish a system of communication and feedback whereby your clients will have immediate access to you and answers to their questions should the need arise. It is incumbent on managers to stay in constant communication with their clients. It is a good idea to set dates and times for you and your clients to get together to discuss matters as they relate to your goals, objectives, plans, and how things are being accomplished.

Always be prepared to research and get the answers to those questions that you may not have the answers to. Some of your feedback and communication may be done through nonverbal communication as well. In fact, a large amount of your interpersonal communication will be accomplished nonverbally. Your writing skills will be key to feedback and your written feedback should be put into outline form before putting it in writing. This will give you an opportunity to look at how well your thoughts and points are organized. Overall, feedback is the most effective way to reduce differences and misunderstandings that may develop as a result of perception and preconceived expectations. Always set the example for your clients. Setting poor examples may cause communication failures.

Moreover, during your feedback process—which is also known as the after action review (AAR)—you should outline and review each scenario after it has occurred. This will also be the time to make changes or updates to your procedures. Overall, during the after action review you will have the opportunity to identify key areas where you have been successful as a whole. You will also be able to review areas that may reflect negatively on the collective performance, which may allow you to make the suitable corrections immediately. Though being proactive may prove to be a more successful approach to management, having the ability to react appropriately and in a timely fashion can prove effective as well. In addition, having a process for proper feedback and review can also assist you with your follow-up by providing you with the appropriate information required in order to specify address issues or concerns that may arise. Furthermore, the feedback and review process may provide you with an opportunity to share quality time with your clients, which may otherwise be interrupted as a result of various commitments and responsibilities.

Generally, these meetings may spark several questions that may require additional follow-up for specific answers. It will be imperative that you keep your clients informed and that you consistently follow-up on leads, submissions, special interests, requests, concerns, and all matters related to assuring and securing the best interests of your clients. By doing so, this can aid you and give you the opportunity to be specifically equipped to effectively represent your clients and their best interests. In addition, your feedback and follow-up process can also result in you being prepared with the knowledge required to effectuate various propositions that you may receive on behalf of your clients. There will be no substitute for your ability to make the correct assessments and decisions on behalf of your clients. Moreover, helping your clients make the right choices and decisions as a result of providing sound and quality advice should always be a part of your primary focus. You should always attempt to provide and maintain an environment for good communication, feedback, and follow-up with your clients. Ultimately, this will lead to your ability to make, and assist your clients with making the appropriate decisions.

Propositions and Decisions

"Knowing is half the battle."

During the course of your management career, you will be faced with several propositions related to the careers of your clients. Each proposition will require you to make decisions and recommendations that may be immensely important to your clients' careers. You may quickly realize that each of the topics previously outlined will assist you a great deal when it comes to how you react and respond to various propositions. Again, the more you know and the more astute you are, the better your chances of making the appropriate decisions. Your ability to assess and make accurate decisions will involve a culmination of the topics outlined. In general, the rate and consistency at which you approach management, multiplied by the amount of time you spend doing it, will produce your distance and desired outcome. Ultimately, your outcome will be a manifestation of your management and decision-making skills. Often, your decisions related to the propositions that you receive will be determined by your goals, desires, and ambitions. Again, always keep in mind that it is your job to aid your clients with accomplishing their objectives, which should always be considered above your own.

Your loyalty and dedication to your clients may be tested on a regular basis, so don't be alarmed by the propositions you may receive, which may seem to question your integrity, honesty, or commitment to your clients. This may become more common than you would expect. Overall, the bonds you form with your clients will support you during this process. Be careful to review each proposition with a wide view and mindset. This may be accomplished by factoring various possibilities and outcomes that may occur as a result of the decisions you may be required to make. For example, one particular proposition may offer your client more money than another. However, you may decide and advise your client that it would be in his or her best interest to accept the proposition offering less money, based on other factors such as the relationship you have with the person or company making the offer, and additional perks your client may receive as a result of accepting this particular offer instead.

In general, deals that are based purely on money often turn out to be mere transactions and don't always account for the "what if contingency." Again, it may not be possible to forecast every potential nuance that can occur. However, looking at each proposition with a broad overview can help you to consider many different factors. You may consider viewing each proposition by attempting to forecast what it will amount to ten or twenty years from the time it is being offered. This may help you and your clients to take a futuristic look at how a decision you make today will affect many tomorrows to come.

On one hand, many of the propositions you receive may not require a great deal of consideration or compromise. They may be a little more simplistic in nature, and thus can be addressed a little less urbane than others. On the other hand, many of the propositions you receive may require legal counsel and review. It is a good practice to advise your clients to have everything reviewed by their attorneys before signing it—no matter what! This may help to address any areas that may be unclear or unspecified within the proposal. It may also serve to protect your clients' interests as a whole. As aforementioned, if your clients are protected, in essence, you will be as well. Overall, you should attempt to make calculated and un-hasty decisions regarding each proposition that you receive. Also, you should make it a point to practice patience when considering and reviewing a proposition, and you should allot plenty of time for a thorough and concise analysis of each offer. Again, making accurate decisions on behalf of your clients will be enormously important.

Obviously, your ability to review and react appropriately may be imperative in many instances throughout. Not only will this fact be important regarding the propositions and decisions you make thereby, but it will also be an important factor that will be factored into all 10 steps towards successfully managing artists. As you grow and continually review these steps, you may adapt your own measures and tactics that may ultimately enhance those already outlined. This may provide your foundation and serve to propel your management career, which may ultimately cast an indelible impression on your lifetime in artist management.

About the Author

Cappriccieo M. Scates is Director of Operations for Precision Management Incorporated/Mytrell Publishing (BMI). Precision Management Inc. is a multilevel music entertainment company that provides Artist Management, Song Placement, Artist & Repertoire, Publishing, Marketing, and Industry Consultation Services.

Mr. Scates' career in artist representation and management has been very successful with a proven track record. He has consulted companies such as: Sony/550, Columbia, Warner Brothers, Bad Boy Entertainment, Atlantic, Motown, Maverick, Death Row, Tommy Boy, A&M, Universal, and several others. In 1996, he was independently contracted as Director of National Radio Promotions for Ruffhouse/Columbia Records where he worked with the likes of the Fugees, Cypress Hill, and Kris Kross. In addition, he has been responsible for promoting the careers of artist such as: Juvenile, New Edition, BlackStreet, Sounds of Blackness, Kim Burrell, Coolio, Meat Loaf, Shai, All 4 One, Bone Thugs-n-Harmony, Luke, Boyz II Men, Eazy E, Lost Boyz, Jon B, Rebbie Jackson, Erykah Badu, and N.O.R.E.

Mr. Scates completed his Associates Degree in Liberal Arts at Saint Leo University and his Bachelor of Arts in Criminology/Sociology there as well where he graduated with a 3.4 GPA. In addition, he holds a Masters Degree in Business Administration from Averett University where he graduated with a 3.8 GPA and was selected to the 2003-2004 National Dean's List for academic excellence. He is currently a Law School Student at Concord University School of Law and a member of the 2004 National Registers Who's Who in Executives and Professionals. He enjoys playing bass guitar, drums, basketball, football, and working with youth.

Readers can contact the author by email at: cappriccieo@pmmusicgroup.com, or by visiting: www.pmmusicgroup.com.

APPENDIX

Staying On Point

10 Ethical Principles

1. Pursuit of Excellence

2. Respect

3. Responsible Citizenship

4. Accountability

5. Honesty

6. Caring

7. Loyalty

8. Integrity

9. Fairness

10. Courtesy

Principles of Ethical Decision Making

*Know Ethical Problem *Know Goal of Your Job* Know The Rules *Consider All People Your Decision Affects *Know All The Facts *Commit To The Best Ethical Solution *Implement Ethical Solution

Motivational Quotes

- "If you don't go after what you want, you'll never have it, If you don't ask, the answer is always no. If you don't step forward, you're always in the same place." Nora Roberts

- "Don't look back, unless you want to go back." Phil Harbolt

- "Success is to be measured not so much by the position that one has reached in life as by the obstacles which he has overcome." Booker T. Washington

- "Every adversity, every failure, every heartache carries with it the seed of an equal or greater benefit." Napoleon Hill

- "Do not fear the winds of adversity. Remember, a kite rises against the wind rather than with it." Unknown Author

- "The greatest mistake you can make in life is to be continually fearing you will make one." Elbert Hubbard

- "Don't wear your problem on your face, no matter the situation. Be cheerful always because your smile can brighten somebody's day and attract solutions to your problem." Bishop Leonard Umunna

- "In any moment of decision, the best thing you can do is the right thing. The worst thing you can do is nothing." Theodore Roosevelt

- "My interest is in the future, because I'm going to be spending the rest of my life there." Charles Kettering

- "Things work out best for the people who make the best out of the way things work out." Art Linkletter

- "When I was a young man I observed that nine out of the ten things I did were failures. Not wanting to be a failure, I did ten times more work." Roosevelt

- "The best way to predict the future is to create it!" Jason Kaufmann

- "Insecurity breeds greatness. To get to the top in virtually anything today, you really have to make a superhuman effort. You won't ever find a super achiever anywhere who wasn't or isn't motivated, at least partially, by a sense of insecurity." Ted Turner

- "Nurture your mind with great thoughts, for you will never go any higher than you think…" Benjamin Disraeli

- "The only difference between a good day and a bad day is your ATTITUDE!" Dennis S. Brown

- "Success is achieved and maintained by those who TRY, and keep TRYING. Where there is nothing to lose by TRYING, and a great deal to gain if SUCCESSFUL, by all means, TRY. DO IT NOW!" W. Clement Stone

- "The future belongs to those who believe in the beauty of their dreams." Eleanor Roosevelt

- "The bitterest tears shed over graves are for words left unsaid and deeds left undone." Harriet Beecher Stowe

- "The ultimate measure of a man is not where he stands in moments of comfort, but were he stands at times of challenge and controversy." Martin Luther King

- "Great minds have purposes, others have wishes." Washington Irving

- "Most successful men have not achieved distinction by having some new talent or opportunity presented to them. They have developed the opportunity that was at hand." Bruce Barton

- "I do not believe in a fate that falls on men however they act, but I do believe in a fate that falls on men unless they act." G.K. Chesterton

- "Know the true value of time; snatch, seize, and enjoy every moment of it. No idleness, no delay, no procrastination; never put off till tomorrow what you can do today." Earl of Chesterfield

- "The greatest thing in this world is not so much where we are, but in which direction we are moving." Oliver Wendell Holmes, Jr.

- "Don't try to be great at all things. Pick a few things to be good at and be the best you can." Liz Ashe

Recommended Readings

All You Need To Know About The Music Business—Donald S. Passman

Confessions of A Record Producer—Moses Avalon

Everything You'd Better Know About the Record Industry—Gary Greenberg and Kashif

Hit Men: Power Brokers and Fast Money Inside the Music Business—Fredric Dannen

Take Care of Your Music Business—John P. Kellogg

The 48 Laws of Power—Robert Greene

The Art of War—Sun Tzu

The Management Methods of Jesus—Bob Briner

The Men Behind Def Jam—Russell Simmons

This Business of Artist Management—Xavier M. Frascogna Jr. and H. Lee Hetherington

This Business of Music—M. William Krasilovsky, John M. Gross, and Sidney Schemel

Who Moved My Cheese—Kenneth Blanchard

Recommended Reference Books

Billboard International Talent and Touring Directory

Hollywood Music Industry Directory

Recording Industry Sourcebook

Songwriter's Market

The Bible

Organizations, Unions, and Guilds

American Federation of Musicians (AFM)
www.afm.org
1501 Broadway Suite 600
NY, NY 10036
(212) 869-1330

American Federation of Television and Radio Artists (AFTRA)
www.aftra.org
260 Madison Ave.
NY, NY 10016
(212) 532-0800

American Guild of Variety Artist (AGVA)
184 5th Ave.
NY, NY 10010
(212) 675-1003

American Society of Composers Authors and Publishers (ASCAP)
www.ascap.com
One Lincoln Plaza
NY, NY 10023
(212) 595-3050

Billboard
www.billboard.com
770 Broadway
NY, NY 10003
(646) 654-4400

Broadcast Music Incorporated (BMI)
www.bmi.com
320 West 57th St.
NY, NY 10019
(212) 586-2000

8730 Sunset Blvd. 3rd Floor West
L.A., CA. 90069
(310) 656-9109

10 Music Square East
Nashville, TN 37203
(615) 401-2000

Conference of Personal Managers
1650 Broadway Suite 705
NY, NY 10019
(212) 265-3366

10231 Riverside Dr. Suite 303
Toluca Lake, CA. 91602
(818) 762-6276

Country Music Association (CMA)
www.cmaworld.com
1 Music Circle South
Nashville, TN 37203
(615) 244-2840

Yellow Pages of Rock
120 North Victory Blvd. Third Floor
Burbank, CA 91501
(818) 955-4000

Gospel Music Association (GMA)
www.gospelmusic.org
1205 Division St.
Nashville, TN 37203
(615) 242-0303

Music Manager Forum (MMF)
www.mmfus.org
P.O. Box 444 Village Station
NY, NY 10014
(212) 213-8787

Music Performance Trust Funds
1501 Broadway Suite 202
NY, NY 10017
(212) 391-3950

National Academy of Recording Arts and Sciences (NARAS)
www.grammy.org
156 W. 56th St. Suite 1701
NY, NY 10019
(212) 245-5440

3402 Pico Blvd.
Santa Monica, CA. 90405
(310) 392-3777

Rap Coalition
www.rapcoalition.org
111 E. 14th St. Suite 339
NY, NY 10003
(212) 714-1100

Recording Industry Association of America (RIAA)
www.riaa.com
1330 Connecticut Ave. NW Suite 300
Washington, D.C. 20036
(202) 775-0101

SESAC
www.sesac.com
55 Music Square East
Nashville, TN 37203
(615) 320-0055

Talent Managers Association (TMA)
www.talentmanagers.org
4804 Laurel Canyon Blvd. Suite 611
Valley Village, CA. 91607
(310) 205-8495

The Harry Fox Agency Incorporated
www.nmpa.org
711 3rd Ave. 8th Floor
NY, NY 10017
(212) 370-5330

The Songwriters Guild if America
www.songwriters.org
1560 Broadway Suite 1306
NY, NY 10036
(212) 768-7902

6430 Sunset Blvd. #1002
Hollywood, CA. 90028
(213) 462-1108

1222 16th Ave. South #25
Nashville, TN 37212
(615) 329-1782

U.S. Copyright Office
www.copyright.gov
Library of Congress
Washington, D.C. 20559
(202) 707-9100

Voter Registration

www.rap-the-vote.org   www.rockthevote.org

Example Management Contract

Company Name and Address

Date:
Artist Name and Address:

Dear Artist Name,

The following when countersigned by you will constitute this the agreement between us with respect to management services to be rendered by us on your behalf.

1. TERM

(Company name) herein (referred to as Manager) is hereby engaged as (artist name) (referred to as Artist) exclusive personal manager and advisor. The agreement shall continue for two (2) years (hereinafter the "initial term") from the date thereof, and shall be renewed for one (1) year periods (hereinafter "renewal period (s)") automatically unless either party shall give written notice of termination to the other not later than thirty (30) days prior to the expiration of the initial term or the current renewal period, as applicable, subject to the terms and conditions hereof.

2. SERVICES

(a) Manager agrees during the term thereof, to advise, counsel, and assist Artist in connection with all matters relating to Artist's career in all branches of the music industry, including without limitation, the following:

(i) in the selection of literary, artistic and musical material;

(ii) with respect to matters pertaining to publicity, promotion, public relations, and advertising;

(iii) with respect to the adoption of proper formats for the presentation of Artist's artistic talents and in determination of the proper style, mood, setting, business, and characterization in keeping with the Artist's talents;

(iv) in the selection of artistic talent to assist, accompany or embellish Artist's artistic presentation, with regard to general practices in the entertainment industries;

(v) with respect to such matters as Manager may have knowledge concerning compensation and privileges extended for similar artistic values;

(vi) with respect to agreements, documents and contracts for Artist's services, and/or artistic, literary, and musical materials.

(vii) with respect to the selection, supervision and coordination of those persons, firms and corporations who may counsel, advise, procure employment, or otherwise render services to or on behalf of Artist, such as accountants, attorneys, business managers, publicists, and talent agents; and

(b) Manager shall be required only to render reasonable services that are called for by this Agreement as and when reasonably requested by Artist. Manager shall not be required to travel or meet with Artist at any particular place or places, expect in Manager's discretion and following arrangements for cost and expenses of such travel, such arrangements to be mutually agreed upon by Artist and Manager.

3. AUTHORITY OF MANAGER

Manager is hereby appointed Artist's exclusive, true and lawful attorney-in-fact, to do any or all of the following, with Artist's prior approval for or on behalf of Artist, during the term of this agreement;

(a) approve and authorize any and all publicity and advertising, subject to Artist's previous approval;

(b) approve and authorize the use of Artist's name, photograph, likeness, voice, sound effects, caricatures, and literary, artistic and musical material for the purpose of advertising any and all products and services, subject to Artist's previous approval;

(c) execute in Artist's name, all contracts for Artist's personal appearances as a live entertainer, subject to Artist's previous consent to the material terms thereof; and

(d) without in anyway limiting the foregoing, generally do, execute and perform any other act, deed, matter or thing whatsoever, that ought to be done on behalf of Artist by a personal manager, subject to Artist's previous approval.

4. COMMISSIONS

(a) Since the nature and extent of the success or failure of Artist's career cannot be predetermined, it is the desire of the parties hereto that Manager's compensation shall be determined in such a manner as will permit Manager to accept the risk of failure as well as the benefit of Artist's success. Therefore, as compensation for Manager's services, Artist shall pay Manager, throughout full term hereof, as when received by Artist, the following percentages of Artist's gross earnings (hereinafter referred to as the "Commission"):

(i) Twenty percent (20%) of Artist's gross earnings providing his or her services as a recording artist for the recording of master recordings to be manufactured and marketed as phonograph records and tapes during the term hereof. Manager shall receive said Commission in perpetuity on the sale of those master recordings recorded during the term hereof. In no event shall the term "gross earnings" be deemed to include payments to third parties, (which are not owned or controlled substantially or entirely by Artist), in connection with the recordings of master recordings prior to or during the term hereof;

(ii) Twenty percent (20%) of Artist's gross earnings from live performances;

(iii) Twenty percent (20%) of the Artist's gross earnings derived from any and all of Artist's activities in connection with music publishing, or licensing or assignment of any compositions composed by Artist alone or in collaboration with others (it being understood that no commissions shall be taken with respect to any compositions that are the subject of any separate music publishing agreement between Artist and Manager);

(b) The term "gross earning" as used herein shall mean and include any and all gross monies or other consideration which Artist may receive, acquire, become entitled to, or which may be payable to Artist, as a direct or indirect result of Manager's services (without any exclusion or deduction) aiding the Artist's activities in the industry, whether as a performer, writer, singer, publisher, or artist.

(c) Manager shall be entitled to receive his full commission as provided herein in perpetuity on Artist's gross earnings derived from any agreement entered into during the term of this agreement, notwithstanding the prior termination of this agreement for any reason. Artist also agrees to pay Manager the commission following the term hereof upon and with respect to all of Artist's gross earnings received after the expiration of term hereof but derived from any and all employment's, engagements, contracts, agreements and activities, negotiated, entered into, commenced or performed during the term hereof relating to any of the foregoing, and upon any resumption's of such employment's, engagements, contracts, agreements, and activities which may have been discontinued during the term hereof and resumed within one (1) year thereafter;

(d) Manager is hereby authorized to receive, on Artist's behalf, all "gross monies and other considerations" and to deposit all such funds into a separate trust account in a bank or savings and loan association. Manager shall have the right to withdraw from such account all expenses and commissions to which manager is entitled hereunder and shall remit the balance to Artist or as Artist shall direct. Notwithstanding the foregoing, Artist may, at any time, require all "gross monies or other considerations" to the paid to a third party, provided that such party shall irrevocably be directed in writing to pay Manager all expenses and commissions due hereunder.

(e) The term "gross monies or other considerations" as used herein shall include, all gross monies derived in connection with Artist or as a direct or indirect result through the involvement of Manager without limitation, salaries, earnings, fees, royalties, bonuses, share of profit and other participation's, partnership interests, or music related percentages, and/or income earned or received directly by Artist or Artist's behalf. Should Artist be required to make any payment for such interest, Manager will pay Manager's percentage share of such payment, unless Manager elects not to acquire Manager's percentage thereof.

5. LOANS AND ADVANCES

Manager will make loans or advances to Artist or for Artist's behalf for the furtherance of Artist's career in amounts to be determined solely by Manager in the Manager's best business judgment. Artist hereby authorizes Manager to recoup and retain the amount of any such loan, advances and/or expenses including, without limitation, transportation and living expenses including traveling, promotion and publicity expenses, all other reasonable and necessary expenses incurred by Manager on behalf of Artist. Artist shall reimburse Manager for any expenses incurred by Manager on behalf of Artist, including, without limitation, long distance calls, and travel expenses. Manager shall incur no single expense in excess of fifty dollars ($50.00) without the prior approval of Artist. If Manager's expenses are incurred regarding services to both Artist and any other clients/Artists, such expenses shall be pro-rated between Artist and Manager's other clients/Artists upon the amount of time Manager rendered its service on behalf of Artist and such other clients/Artists. At no point shall Manager's overhead costs be characterized as expenses reimbursable by Artist. Manager shall provide Artist with monthly statements of all expenses incurred hereunder and Artist shall reimburse Manager within fourteen (14) days of receipt by Artist of any such statement. Artist agrees to reimburse Manager upon demand for all expenses incurred by Manager on Artist's behalf, and any such expenses, which at the time remain unreimbursed, may be deducted by Manager from Artist's Gross Income. Notwithstanding the foregoing, any loans, advances or payment of expenses by Manager hereunder shall not be recoupable by Manager hereunder until Artist has earned revenue in the entertainment industries and there is sufficient such revenue to so recoup, repay, and to compensate Manager without causing Artist hardship or leaving insufficient funds for Artist to pursue his or her career.

6. NON EXCLUSIVITY

Manager's services hereunder are not exclusive. Manager shall at all times be free to perform similar services for others, as well as to engage in any and all other business activities.

7. ARTIST'S CAREER

Artist agrees to pay at all times to pursue Artist's career in a manner consistent with Artist's values, goals, philosophy, and disposition and to do all things necessary and desirable to promote such career and earnings there from. Artist will utilize proper theatrical and other employment agencies to obtain engagements and employment for Artist. Artist shall consult with Manager regarding all offers of employment inquiries concerning Artist's services. Artist shall not, without Managers prior written approval, engage any other person, firm or corporation to render any services of the kind required of Manager hereunder or which Manager is permitted to perform hereunder.

8. ADVERTISING

During the term hereof, Manager shall have the exclusive right to advertise/ publicize Manager as Artist's personal manager and representative with respect to the music industry.

9. ENTIRE AGREEMENT

This constitutes the entire agreement between Artist and Manager relating to the subject matter hereof. This agreement shall be subject to and construed in accordance with laws of the State of (Your State Here) applicable to agreements entered into and fully performed therein. A waiver by either party hereto or a breach of any provision herein shall not be deemed a waiver or any subsequent breach, nor a permanent modification of such provision. Each party acknowledges that no statement, promise or inducement has been made to such party, except as expressly provided for herein. This agreement may not be changed or modified, or in any covenant or provision hereof waived, except by an agreement in writing, signed by the party against whom enforcement of the change, modification or waiver is sought. As used in this agreement, the word "Artist" shall include any corporation owned (partially or wholly) or controlled (directly or indirectly) by Artist and Artist agrees to cause any such corporation to enter into an agreement with Manager of the same terms and conditions contained herein.

10. LEGALITY

Nothing contained in this agreement shall be construed to require the commission of any act contrary to law. Whenever there is any conflict between any provision of this agreement in any material law, contrary to which the parties have no legal right to contract, the latter shall prevail, but in such event the provisions of this agreement affected shall be curtailed and restricted only to the extent necessary to bring in such legal requirements, and only during the time such conflict exists.

11. CONFLICTING INTERESTS

(a) From time to time during the term of this agreement, acting alone or in association with others, Manager may act as the interpreter or promoter of an entertainment program in which Artist is employed by Manager or Manager may employ Artist in connection with the production of photographic records, or as a songwriter, composer or arranger. Such activity on Managers part shall not be deemed to be a breach of this agreement or of Managers obligations and duties to

Artist. However, Manager shall not be entitled to commission in connection with any gross earnings derived by Artist from any employment or agreement where under Artist is employed by Manager, or by firm, person or corporation represented by Manager as the package agent for the entertainment program in which Artist is so employed; and Manager shall not be entitled to the commission in connection with any gross earnings derived by Artist from the sale, license or grant of rights in connection with any entertainment program, phonograph record, or other matter, merely because Manager is also employed in connections there with as a producer, director, conductor or in some other management or supervisory capacity, but not as Artist's employer, grantee or licensee.

(b) It is expressly understood and agreed that Manager is neither an employment agency, a talent or theatrical agency nor a booking agent, and that Manager has not offered or promised to obtain employment or engagements for Artist, and that Manager is not obligated, authorized or expected to do so.

12. SCOPE

This agreement shall not be construed to create a partnership between the parties. Each party is acting hereunder as an independent contractor. Manager may appoint or engage any other persons, firms, or corporations, throughout the world, in Managers discretion, to perform any of the services which Manager has agreed to perform hereunder except that Manager may delegate all of his duties only with Artist's written consent. Manager's services hereunder are not exclusive to Artist and Manager shall at all times be free to perform the same or similar services for others as well as to engage in any and all other business activities. Manager shall only be required to render reasonable services that are provided for herein as and when reasonably requested by Artist. Manager shall not be deemed to be in breach of this agreement unless and until Artist shall first have given Manager written notice describing the exact service which Artist requires on Managers part and then only if Manager is in fact required to render such services hereunder, and if Manager shall thereafter have failed for a period of thirty (30) consecutive days to commence the rendition of the particular service required.

13. ASSIGNMENT

Manager shall have the right to assign this agreement to any and all of Managers rights hereunder, or delegate any and all of Managers duties to any individual, firm or corporation with the written approval of Artist, and this agreement shall inure to the benefit of Managers successors and assigns, provided that Manager shall always be primarily responsible for rendering of managerial services, and may not delegate all of his duties without Artist written consent. This agreement is personal to Artist, and Artist shall not assign this agreement or a portion thereof, in any such purported assignment shall be void.

14. NOTICES

All notices to be given to any of the parties hereto shall be addressed to the respective party at the applicable address as follows: ("Artist") c/o Artist name and address and ("Manager") c/o Company name and address.

All notices shall be in writing and shall be served by mail or telegraph, all charges pre-paid. The date of mailing or of deposit in a telegraphy office, whichever shall be first, shall be deemed the date such notice is effective.

15. ARTIST'S WARRANTIES

Artist represents, warrants and agrees that Artist is over the age of eighteen (18), free to enter into this agreement, and that Artist has not heretofore made and will not hereafter enter into or accept any engagement, commitment or agreement with any person, firm or corporation which will, can or may interfere with the full and faithful performance by Artist of the covenants, terms and conditions of this agreement to be performed by Artist or interfere with Managers full enjoyment of Managers rights and privileges hereunder. Artist warrants that Artist has, as of the date hereof, no commitment, engagement or agreement requiring Artist to render services or preventing Artist from rendering the disposition of any rights which Artist has or may hereafter acquire in any musical composition or creation, and acknowledges that the Artist's talents and abilities are exceptional, extraordinary, and unique, the loss of which cannot be compensated for by money.

16. ARBITRATION

In the event of any dispute under or relating to the terms of this agreement or any breach thereof, it is agreed that the same shall be submitted to arbitration in accordance with the rules promulgated by arbitrator and judgment upon any award rendered by be entered in any court having jurisdiction thereof. In the event of litigation or arbitration arising from or out of this agreement or relationship of the parties creating hereby, the trier thereof may award to any party any reasonable attorney's fees and other costs incurred in connection therewith. Any litigation by Manager or Artist arising from or out of this agreement shall be brought in the State of (Your State Here).

IN WITNESS WHEREOF, the parties hereto have signed this agreement as of the date herein above set forth.

Sincerely,

Representative Name
Company Name

ACCEPTED AND AGREED TO:

_____

Artist Name:
SS#

_____

Witness Name:

IMPORTANT LEGAL DOCUMENT—CONSULT YOUR ATTORNEY BEFORE SIGNING (Example)

Conclusion

Like most things, artist management is what you make of it. At times you must be as gentle as a lamb, but with an ability to become as firm as a lion in an instance. Management can be a lifelong quest. More than likely, it will turnout to be a huge commitment. You will probably experience highs and lows that may keep you on the borders of depression. Most likely, this fact may become routine. Always remember that your floor is someone else's ceiling, and therefore be appreciative of your accomplishments, but keep attempting to reach the next floor.

Most importantly, be aware that there are rules and standards regarding artist management that you should apply with an extreme degree of ethical behavior. The slightest impropriety should be avoided at all costs, if possible. Furthermore, attempt to divest yourself of unwarranted conflicts and be responsible for all of your actions and those of your clients. Keep in mind that you will be faced with the constant challenge of serving as both a supervisor and subordinate while carrying out your daily tasks. Therefore, it will be important for you to keep this fact in perspective. Balancing your life along with your management career will be difficult, but it is attainable. You should always look for the balance between the two.

Lastly, I challenge you to uphold the integrity and fortitude required of all managers. You will be one of the most important aspects of your clients' careers. For that reason, much will be required of you. Stay informed, and remain as proactive as possible. We are the glue that keeps the artist grounded. Don't ever lose sight of your responsibilities. Be, know, and do; you are an **ARTIST MANAGER!**

Note:

"I've always let faith and optimism be the determining factors behind my success. I've never been afraid to take risks, or to trust in my own abilities to succeed. At the end of the day, it's important to me that I've tried my best, and have given all that I could to be an effective and successful manager."

Cappriccieo M. Scates, M.B.A. (J.D. Candidate)
Author

0-595-32851-2